MW00723275

MOSTLY OVERLOOKED

SECRETS

OF

LLCS

CHRISTINE E. CASSIDY, CPA, JD, LLM

Copyright © 2021
COWCATCHER Publications
CHRISTINE E. CASSIDY, CPA, JD, LLM
The Little Black Book of
MOSTLY OVERLOOKED SECRETS OF LLCS
All rights reserved.

No part of this publication may be reproduced, distributed, or transmitted in any form or by any means, including photocopying, recording, or other electronic or mechanical methods, without the prior written permission of the publisher, except in the case of brief quotations embodied in critical reviews and certain other non-commercial uses permitted by copyright law.

COWCATCHER Publications
Hilton Head, South Carolina

Printed in the United States of America
First Printing 2021
First Edition 2021

ISBN 978-0-9975172-8-6

Cover Illustration and Design: COWCATCHER Publications

The information provided herein is stated to be truthful and consistent, in that any liability, in terms of inattention or otherwise, by any usage or abuse of any policies, processes, or direction contained within is the solitary responsibility of the recipient reader. Under no circumstances will any legal responsibility or blame be held against the publisher for any reparations, damages, or monetary loss due to the information herein, either directly or indirectly. The information herein in offered solely for informational purposes. Additionally, the publisher does not intend text to serve as legal advice. If you are seeking legal advice, please contact an attorney who is well-versed in business law.

The Little Black Book of

MOSTLY OVERLOOKED SECRETS OF LLCS

TABLE OF CONTENTS

A NOTE FROM THE AUTHOR

"Know what you are getting into and then make the most of it."

Chris Cassidy, CPA, JD, LLM

This book was written to give readers a basic understanding of the business entity known as a Limited Liability Company, or an LLC. My hope is that you will gain an understanding why LLCs have become the entity of choice for so many business owners. I also include a discussion of the various tax structures that affect LLCs, namely, sole proprietorships, partnerships, and corporations. By the end, you will understand how the two work together, and that will be a great help in deciding which structure to use for your business.

This Little Black Book is a distillation of forty years of experience as both a tax attorney and a CPA. Typically, my clients have been businesses in a variety of industries with a net worth of $1m to $10m. I also help individuals, estates and trusts of similar net worth.

Of course, I've helped many clients with much less wealth as well. My goal is to help clients successfully create a durable foundation upon which their business can flourish. Removing hidden obstacles, research and planning—this is where I excel. Over the years, I've enjoyed playing a small part of helping business owners fulfill their dreams. I have been very fortunate to have been part of many wonderful dreams.

INTRODUCTION

Hardly anyone noticed when, in 1977, the state of Wyoming passed legislation allowing a new type of company called a Limited Liability Company (LLC). Today, over two-thirds of all new companies formed are LLCs.

Nowadays, when someone wants to start a business, the first question that arises is, "Should I establish my business as an LLC?" Why is that? I believe it is because there is a vague notion an LLC is helpful and necessary, but most people have no idea what the advantages or disadvantages of forming an LLC are. I can help with that.

Vague notion #1: An LLC can protect me, but from what exactly?

Vague notion #2: An LLC will make things easier, but what things exactly?

Vague notion #3: An LLC will save me from paying too much in taxes, but how exactly?

Here is a list of questions I hear when someone consults with me about starting or rebuilding a business.

- How does an LLC protect me from creditors?
- How are LLCs taxed?
- Can I establish an LLC myself, or do I need a lawyer or a registered agent?
- Where should I establish my LLC?
- If someone else is involved, what will an LLC do for our relationship?
- What happens if I want to disconnect from an LLC?
- When compared to other business structures, such as sole proprietorships, limited partnerships, C Corporations, S Corporations, and joint ventures, what are the advantages and disadvantages of an LLC?

You must understand how an LLC functions to know whether it is the best business structure for your enterprise. I will address all those questions and more. But why listen to me? What advice can I offer that will provide the confidence you need to move forward?

One mostly overlooked secret to success is that victory is often buried within the minute details of a business plan; and, while some people don't enjoy sorting through tedious details, I do. I'm at my best when I'm helping business owners establish a sturdy foundation for a more secure future. Let's face it. Some people prefer to jump ahead and sell the lemonade rather than figure out how to protect assets in order to reach and maintain a sustainable future. I make sure people know what they're getting into so they can make the most of their pursuits.

 Just so you know, I'm certified to practice before the US Tax Court.

PART ONE

WHAT EXACTLY IS AN LLC, AND WHAT ARE ITS TWO MAIN BENEFITS?

Limited liability companies are state-created organizations. If you are reading this you are in the process of deciding what kind of organization is best for your business. You already have a sound personal understanding of how your business operates and what it needs to be profitable. This is the next step—how do I protect it in terms of liability and tax? You are on the right path if you are considering an LLC.

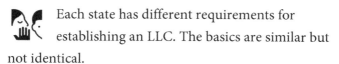 Each state has different requirements for establishing an LLC. The basics are similar but not identical.

Think of the LLC as a bunker which houses and protects your business assets and operations. If your main objective is to create a vehicle that will sensibly manage your liability and tax concerns while making enough money to support yourself and your family, then an LLC is probably right for you. Here is why.

Whatever happens in the bunker, whatever liabilities the business incurs as well as whatever debts or claims are assigned to the business, belongs to and stays within the bunker. There are exceptions, of course, but generally, business problems stay in the bunker. Creditors will have a difficult time coming after the assets in the LLC, including personal assets, when there is a problem. However, there are important exceptions.

PROTECTION FOR YOURSELF AND YOUR ASSETS

The name itself—limited liability company—implies its biggest advantage. An LLC protects its owners, members, managers, and the LLC from certain types of liability. When I say protected, I mean the owners and their personal assets are not liable for claims against the LLC. Additionally, the LLC assets are insulated from claims against the LLC. There is a double layer of protection, meaning both the owner's personal assets and the LLC's assets are protected.

But not everything is protected. Let's go through what is protected and what is not. The following points discuss specific ways in which your personal assets can be threatened and how they are safeguarded by the LLC bunker.

1.   **PERSONAL LIABILITY FOR LLC DEBTS** If you form an LLC, and it incurs debt, you as the owner are not responsible for the payment of the debts. The bank has no ability to go after you and your personal assets for payment. It cannot force you to relinquish any of your personal assets, such as bank accounts or investments. Most states have this law but there are exceptions so you will have to check your state laws. There is one exception. Do not personally guarantee the debt or you will be liable. For example, if the LLC borrowed $100,000 from a bank, and the LLC cannot make the payments, and you personally guaranteed the debt, the bank will come after you. A guarantee is a separate agreement you sign which says that you will pay in case your LLC does not.

AVOID PERSONAL GUARANTEES IF YOU CAN

Creditors and plaintiffs are limited in their recovery efforts when dealing with an LLC. This limitation is ruined if you personally guarantee the debt. A personal guarantee is where you agree separately with the bank, for example, that should the LLC not pay its debts, you will. In many cases, this is hard to avoid. A bank can decide not to lend money to the LLC unless you personally guarantee the debt. You can attempt to restrict the guaranteed agreement to various events, but this may not work in some situations. The LLC will not get the loan unless the owner or owners personally guarantee the debt. The only thing you can do is to make sure your spouse does not sign the guarantee.

 LITTLE ASSET PROTECTION TIP If you do get stuck with a personally guaranteed LLC debt, or your lender requires personal guarantees of LLC debt, remember that only your assets are subject to the guarantee. It may be time to do some family and estate planning. This would include re-titling assets to a family LLC or some other entity. This would take those assets off the liability table.

2.   **PERSONAL LIABILITY FOR ACTIONS OF YOUR CO-MEMBERS OR EMPLOYEES** If a co-member or employee is involved in wrongdoing and there is a judgment of some kind, the LLC can be called upon to satisfy the judgment, but not you or your personal assets. For example, if a co-member is found to be responsible for theft from one or more of your

customers, the LLC may have to repay. You would not be personally responsible to satisfy the judgement.

3. **THE PERSONAL DEBTS OF ITS MEMBERS**
The LLC is not responsible for the personal debts of its co-owner, managers, or members.

4. **PERSONAL LIABILITY FOR YOUR OWN ACTIONS** You will always be responsible for your own misdeeds. This means that if you injure someone during the course of doing business, commit some unprofessional act in a service LLC, fail to deposit taxes or intentionally commit a fraudulent or illegal act in the course of business, *you will be personally responsible*. The LLC does not protect you from negligence, malpractice, or other personal wrongdoing. You can be sued and be required to satisfy any judgment with your personal assets. For example, if you are an attorney doing business as an LLC and you commit malpractice, the victim can sue the LLC, which will be paid, no doubt, from an insurance policy purchased by the LLC. However, you could also be liable for satisfying the judgment using your personal assets.

5.   **PIERCING THE CORPORATE VEIL** Any of the above protections can be lost if you do not maintain the separation between you and the LLC. For example, if you have been using the LLC's bank account to pay personal expenses on a regular basis, this interrupts the separation. Because you used the LLC as your personal bank account, and therefore lost the distinction, you could be required to pay any debt by liquidating personal assets.

6.   **CHARGING ORDER PROTECTION** This is an entirely different kind of protection that I consider icing on the cake. It's best explained using an example. Let's say you're a real estate broker transporting clients to view some properties and you have an accident on the way and your clients are hurt. As a result, you are sued. The case goes to trial and the jury finds in favor of your client and asks that you pay for damages in excess of your insurance coverage.

 The plaintiff will execute against your personal assets, one of which, if it's stock in your company, will be a problem. As a personal asset, it is within the plaintiff's reach. The plaintiff can step into your company through ownership of your stock. At that point, it's possible the plaintiff could take full control of the company's assets and you have just lost your business.

Instead, let's say you have established the real estate brokerage as an LLC and the same thing happens. There is the judgment and an execution against your LLC's interest. The outcome will be hugely different. The plaintiff cannot step in the shoes of ownership. All they can do is get a charging order against any distributions, cash or otherwise, coming from your LLC. They cannot force you to make distributions and have no say at all in the business. They can only wait for a distribution out of the LLC to satisfy the judgment. Some states have the charging order as an exclusive remedy, and some do not. In some states, a charging order may not be exclusive, yet it still carries a lot of protection. If possible, I would prefer a state that makes this protection exclusive.

LLCs ARE EASIER TO OPERATE THAN CORPORATIONS

Unlike an LLC, corporations have strict rules on management and recordkeeping. Records of shareholder decisions and actions must be kept in the form of minutes and included in corporate information. The corporation operates according to its bylaws, which are the rules instituted at formation. They have a board of directors and depending upon what the shareholders have agreed to, only the board can make important management and financial decisions.

Corporations must keep financial records. Depending on the size of the organization and its agreements, shareholders are given reports through audits or other third-party reviews. It is a complex structure with lots of requirements, all designed to protect the owners from the corporation. These rules create the image that the corporation is its own distinct entity and acts according to its agreed upon rules, not according to the directives of its owners. Protection is forfeited if these rules are not followed.

The second main advantage of operating as an LLC is the amount of flexibility that comes with the organization's operations. There's no requirement to adopt a board of directors or to elect officers if you so choose. There are no annual meeting requirements and no strict rules about bookkeeping records. You can structure and develop your own method of how things will be managed. You can choose managers among the owners of the LLC, or you can choose a separate non-owner management group to run the company.

The LLC should at least have an operating agreement that sets out the rules and regulations much like the corporate bylaws, but the rules are up to the owners. States do differ but owners can set the rules rather than the state. This goes so far as to say the operating agreement can be oral or written. However, I strongly suggest having a written operating agreement for when the disputes arise; and trust me, they will arise. It's a question of when, not if. Having an operating agreement in place will serve you well and prevent a lot of headaches.

Let's be clear. LLCs are not corporations, yet they have some similarities. For example, an LLC and a corporation are legal entities separate from the owners.

The assets of a corporation as well as the assets of an LLC and the owners' personal assets are separate. C corporation owners and an LLC owners' assets cannot be attached to pay corporate or LLC debts. Owners are not liable for corporate or LLC debts.

This complexity does not exist with an LLC. You can make your own management rules without a board of directors or formal record keeping. You can do all of this and still have protection of your personal assets, which is key. You get the same protection with fewer rules and regulations.

PART TWO

LET'S GET STARTED

ARTICLES OF ORGANIZATION

Each state has specific requirements for establishing an LLC. These organizations operate under state law, which is why you should be aware of these state regulations. There is a misconception that you must pick the state in which you do business. That is not correct. It's more accurate to say you should pick the state whose statute is the most favorable to what you want to do and how you want to file your taxes.

This could be your home state, but it does not have to be. For example, many owners choose to file in Delaware because the Delaware Limited Liability Statute offers the most flexibility in management, such as good faith requirements among the owners and restrictions on voting. You can do business in South Carolina and use a Delaware limited liability statute. Choose the state law that will govern your LLC in the manner you prefer. Again, it has nothing to do with where you do business.

The formation of an LLC begins with the filing of Articles of Organization, which is a two-to-three-page document. You select a name for the LLC and then add a registered agent. This is someone, not necessarily yourself, who has an address in the state in which you choose to file and can receive state correspondence. You pick an organizer which is the name of the person filing for the articles. This not the registered agent.

You also pick the longevity of the LLC. This is only the document that announces to the state that this entity has been formed. Period. It includes the name of the entity, the name and official address of the registered agent, and the name of the person who has organized the entity or is filing these articles. The cost of filing is usually minimal. For example, South Carolina has no annual filing requirement. Such states as Delaware and California, however, have filing requirements and fees.

Let's say John is running an automotive business and has equipment, an inventory of auto parts, and employees on his payroll. He decides to become an LLC. He will file the Articles of Organization, and once they've been approved, he will transfer the equipment, bank account, and employees to the LLC. Everything related to his payroll is now maintained within the

LLC. His EIN (Employer Identification Number) for the old business becomes the EIN of the LLC. John could also get a new EIN for the LLC. In essence, the LLC is now the owner of the operations. John owns the LLC's interest and the bunker that owns the equipment and operations.

LLCs are state law creations, and therefore, the rules can vary from state to state. The following are the general steps you would take to form the LLC. It begins with the filing of the Articles of Organization.

1.   **Pick a name.** The options are unlimited. Use the name you like, which hopefully is unique, as well as the distinct address of the real estate that will be in the LLC. Don't use a long name as that gets complicated on documents. After the name, you are required to have the designation, LLC. For example, the name would read John's Automotive, LLC. Once you have the name, you can now apply for Articles of Organization. Some refer to this document as the Articles of Formation. It means the same. Both terms refer to you, the LLC. Check the state's website to find out if the name you've chosen is being used elsewhere. In South Carolina, the website's address would be

www.SOS.SC.gov. SOS stands for Secretary of State. If the name is available, go to the next step.

2.   **Add the name of the registered agent and their address**. This is the address the state will use to send administrative information. You will decide the term of life for the LLC and who is the organizer, usually the person filing for the Articles. In fact, there is no place on the form to designate who owns the LLC. That information is disclosed in the operating agreement. For most states there is no owner designation on the Articles of Organization. Once you've filled out the Articles of Organization, you would most likely file them online. You now have the first prong of your LLC.

3.   **Who will manage your organization?** This decision, either member-managed or manager-managed, is simple. If the members themselves will manage the business (in other words, will decide what the daily operations of the business will look like), then the LLC will be member-managed. If you have a management group that will manage (make operational decisions), then the LLC is a manager-managed LLC. More about this later.

After completing these steps, the bones of your LLC have taken shape. However, there are other requirements. You will need to start a bank account for the LLC. All income and expenses must be run through that account. In most states, opening a bank account also requires a copy of the operating agreement, which is the document that provides the names of the owners. More about the Operating Agreement coming up.

HOW TO DECIDE WHICH STATE TO USE

You do not have to form your LLC in the state of your residence. You could be a California resident and decide to form the LLC in Delaware. Or you could be a Florida resident and form your LLC in South Carolina. How do you decide?

You pick the state that has the best LLC statute for your purpose. Not all states are equivalent in their laws. Delaware, for example, allows you to remove all fiduciary duties to your members. Another state may not. One state may allow you to assign very extensive management rights to minority members and another may not.

The point is that state law will regulate your relationship with other members and third parties. Pick the state whose law gives you the most flexibility. It may not be your home state, and that still works.

Here's an example. Jill and Terry, both licensed South Carolina real estate agents, want to start a real estate brokerage company. They want to work together in the brokerage business but have their own clients as well. This means they could very well be in competition with each other on some real estate transactions. They would like to have a SC LLC, but the SC statute will probably require much more good faith and fiduciary responsibility on the part of both agents.

The brokerage business could make taking on their own contracts a breach if they don't offer their individual contracts to the brokerage. Jill and Terry want complete freedom to make that choice. They can, and should, put a provision in their operating agreement that addresses this situation, but the state of South Carolina may not consider that enforceable. However, if they established their LLC in Delaware, they could have that provision in the operating agreement, which would be endorsed by the state of Delaware.

Jill and Terry's decision has very little to do with taxes. They will pay state income tax in the state in which their business is earning income. It may not be the state where they filed for their LLC. To clarify, Jill and Terry started their real estate brokerage business in South Carolina, where all of their income is earned. They established their LLC in Delaware. They will report no income to the state of Delaware since no income was earned there. Also, Jill and Terry considered the fact that Delaware deals with creditor issues in a more beneficial way than South Carolina. Because of these factors, Jill and Terry decided it would be best to charter their LLC in Delaware.

PART THREE

LLC OWNERSHIP EXPLAINED

MEMBERS

An LLC refers to its owners as members. Members can be individuals, partnerships, or corporations. The actual number of owners does not matter, meaning the total number of members in an LLC can be large or small.

Owners receive a membership interest in the LLC by contributing something the LLC deems useful to the business. In most cases, this is cash, some type of service or expertise (time), equipment, or property. Owners are issued a membership interest upon the receipt of their contribution.

The value of a member's contribution, when compared to the total value of the LLC, will determine a member's percentage of ownership. In smaller LLCs, members can decide values and percentages. This doesn't have to be anything exceedingly formal.

For example, Bob and Jim have decided they will operate their lawncare business with an even fifty-fifty ownership split. Bob contributes $10,000 in cash while Jim contributes his time and expertise. This means Bob and Jim recognize that Jim's time and expertise is worth $10,000. Because Bob and Jim's LLC is small, this can be established in an informal discussion. However, in a larger LLC with many members and large amounts of capital, there is a more formal method of calculating the value of capital, which can be negotiated among members.

Whether a small or large LLC, members must decide upon the following:

1. How profits will be allocated to members.

2. How members will get cash out of the business.

3. Who makes financial decisions.

4. How to admit new members.

5. What to do when a member wants to withdraw from the LLC.

THE OPERATING AGREEMENT

 The above-mentioned issues must be addressed in the operating agreement, which becomes the LLC's "rules of the road". Think of the operating agreement as the code of conduct and roadmap for success.

Most people either ignore this step or decide to prepare it down the road when it's too late. The operating agreement should be prepared when the Articles of Organization are filed and when everyone is excited about the new business.

 People are more inclined to cooperate with each (and think more clearly) before they must face issues that will most likely surface down the road.

This document is called the operating agreement because everyone involved will be satisfied knowing that relationships and duties in the association have been clearly defined.

In my experience, I can guarantee that as the LLC starts operating and decisions must be made, problems will arise, which is why putting an operating agreement in writing is the wise thing to do. Most states require the agreement to be in writing while other states acknowledge the validity of oral agreements.

 Be sure to check your state's statues. If the situation is not stipulated in your LLC's operating agreement, the state's LLC statute will decide for you.

KEY PROVISIONS OF AN OPERATING AGREEMENT

1.   **Opening Paragraph**: Everyone must agree as to where the business will be operating (location) and the name of the LLC. The opening paragraph should also include a description of the business and a reference to its owners. Lastly, there should be a note as to how the LLC will be treated for tax purposes. Part Four explains tax implications in more detail.

2.   **Duration:** The Articles of Organization commonly select an "at will" period of duration, which stands for" in perpetuity". However, lenders often require an LLC to specify its duration term, such as 50 years.

3.   Ownership and Capital: The operating agreement should clearly state how a member's contribution will be valued and what kind of ownership percentage their contribution provides. As stated earlier, ownership percentage is equal to the contribution made over total contribution and value of the LLC. This calculation should be included here in the operating agreement. Describe how to value time and equipment. If it is done by negotiation, explain the parameters here. Also, this is where loans to members should be clarified. Can the LLC even make loans to members? There should also be provision about what happens when additional capital is needed and how the LLC will acquire it.

4.   **Method of Accounting**: Everyone should be on the same page about how net income will be calculated. After all, members are allocated their portion and then required to pay tax on it, which is why everyone should agree regarding the formula that will be used. There are several different accounting methods, which goes beyond this discussion, but is still an important consideration. Consult a tax advisor to make sure you've chosen the best method for your needs.

5.   Profit and Loss: Members need to know how profit and loss will be allocated. After all, people go into business for the benefits, one of which is the profitable return on their investment. This section can be very straightforward. For example, a 50% member and will receive 50% of the profits and losses. The situation is more complex when a member has contributed more than other members. Initially, that member will receive more profit until they are paid back, after which everyone will share 50/50. This is called a preferential allocation of profit. Again, this section reflects the agreement reached by its members.

6.   **Cash Distributions:** It is a big mistake to think profits equal cash. A business can have $50,000 of profit without distributing any cash. For example, let's say Jill is a 20% member of an LLC. The profit this year is $100,000, therefore, Jill's share of the profit is $20,000, but she did not receive any cash. How can that happen? Cash is low because of the business expenses that didn't enter the calculation of profit. One example would be if the LLC decided to pay down debt. This is called "phantom income," something members may not necessarily want but should be made aware of. Management will make decisions concerning cash distributions.

7.   Management: Choosing a management structure is the most important decision members make. By and large, LLC's have a simple management structure. LLCs do not have a board of directors and they do not have to have a management team. Members need to decide who has the final say or things will be chaotic. Who manages the cash? Who oversees hiring vendors and makes all of the other day to day decisions? Ultimately, the LLC will be either member-managed or manager-managed. Member-managed is where members designate various member responsibilities. Manager-managed is where members elect or hire a manager to conduct the affairs of the business. The manager may or may not be a member of the LLC. It would be wise to stipulate how to replace a manager or management team, whether they would be indemnified for costly decisions, and what to do when and if the LLC is sued because of a manager's bad decision.

Key management decisions include:

1.   Should the LLC take out a loan, and, if so, what terms are acceptable?

2.   How much working capital should the LLC retain?

3.   When and how will the LLC distribute cash?

4. When and how should the LLC take on new members?

5. Which vendors to use, what kind of insurance policies are necessary, and who to hire as an accountant, etc.

8. Transfers: The operating agreement should stipulate what happens when a member leaves or dies. In other word, how will the member's interest be valued coming in or going out? When a member dies, it must be determined how and if the LLC will satisfy the estate of the deceased.

 BEWARE: The state's limited liability statute will apply if there is no agreement as to how to get out of the LLC.

For example, if the agreement says that the LLC will pay the estate of a deceased member the value of their interest, and unfortunately that is all the agreement said, the state's statue will kick in and require the LLC to pay full market value (FMV) within 90 days of the death. This may be injurious to the LLC if it does not have the ability to come up with those funds within 90 days. More time may be needed; but, because the operating agreement did not address this situation specifically, the state statue will be executed.

BEWARE: Members should think twice if the state's statue says all members owe each other good faith and fiduciary responsibilities.

Let's say John's Automotive, LLC is merging with Joe's auto detailing business. Joe wants to join up with John for some jobs but not others. They both acknowledge that there could be jobs where competition might occur between them. However, there is no provision in the agreement providing for Joe's ability to compete with John's Automotive.

What happens if a detailing job comes up that John considered part of their combined business, but Joe disagrees. If Joe takes a job that is not offered to John's Auto, according to the good faith and fiduciary responsibilities statute, Joe could be in trouble and their dispute will have to be resolved. If competition was not addressed adequately in their operating agreement, the limited liability statute would apply. In other words, answer the question, "Can partners compete?" up front in the Operating Agreement.

PART FOUR

HOW MUCH GOES TO UNCLE SAM

The limited liability company is a legal entity created by statue. It does not have its own tax structure. An LLC is not like a corporation, which is a legal entity automatically taxed as a corporation. It is not like a partnership, which is a legal entity automatically taxed like a partnership.

LET'S START WITH THE ESSENTIALS
Then we'll take a look at tax implications for each entity.

SOLE PROPRIETORSHIP ESSENTIALS

OWNER: Individual
SEPARATE ENTITY: Yes
TAX: Highest, includes social security tax
MANAGEMENT: Easiest because it's just YOU!
CASH DISTRIBUTION: No restrictions.
BEST FOR: Small start-ups and small businesses when the owner wants flexibility.
ASSET PROTECTION: None.
CONVERT TO LLC: File Articles of Conversion. Nontaxable.

SOLE PROPRIETORSHIP TAX IMPLICATIONS

- Profit will be taxed on the owner's IRS FORM 1040.
- Profit, if there is any, is calculated using Schedule C.
- Schedule C is where owner lists income and expenses.
- Owners will pay income and social security tax on profits earned.

PARTNERSHIP ESSENTIALS

OWNER: More than one.
SEPARATE ENTITY: Yes.
TAX: Pass-thru entity, includes income and social security taxes.
MANAGEMENT: By agreement, flexible.
CASH DISTRIBUTION: By agreement, with restrictions.
BEST FOR: Partners who want to be treated as a pass-thru entity.
ASSET PROTECTION: Good.
CONVERT TO LLC: File Articles of Conversion, potentially taxable.

PARTNERSHIP TAX IMPLICATIONS

- Profit is calculated on IRS FORM 1065 and split between partners.
- Profit is taxed on IRS FORM 1040.
- Partners pay income and social security tax on profits earned.

S CORPORATION ESSENTIALS

OWNER: One or more.
SEPARATE ENTITY: Yes.
TAX: Pass-thru entity, taxed at the shareholder level with exceptions.
MANAGEMENT: Rigid but less rigid than C corporation.
CASH DISTRIBUTION: With restrictions.
BEST FOR: One or more shareholders who want easy cash distribution and limit what they pay in social security tax.
ASSET PROTECTION: Good.
CONVERT TO LLC: File Articles of Conversion, potentially taxable.

S CORPORATION TAX IMPLICATIONS

- Profit is calculated on IRS FORM 1120-S and split among shareholders.
- Profit is taxed on IRS FORM 1040 on the shareholders' FORM 1040.
- Shareholders pay only income tax.

C CORPORATION ESSENTIALS

OWNER: One or more.
SEPARATE ENTITY: Yes.
TAX: At the corporate level.
MANAGEMENT: Strict rules, rigid and complex.
CASH DISTRIBUTION: Dividends are taxed.
BEST FOR: Multi-member entity, usually large and includes capital investors.
ASSET PROTECTION: Good.
CONVERT TO LLC: File Articles of Conversion, potentially taxable.

C CORPORATION TAX IMPLICATIONS

- The IRS requires C corporations to file Schedule 1020-C, Income Tax Return for Cooperative Associations form.
- Only pays income tax.

If I still have questions, it might be time to call a CPA or a tax attorney.

PART FIVE

CONVERTING TO AN LLC

Let's say you have the following concerns:

- You're starting to worry about creditors and how litigious people are these days.
- You worked hard for many years to develop your business and have acquired personal assets you want to protect.
- You've decided an LLC is the best vehicle to accomplish these objectives.
- You want everything else to stay the same. You don't want the hassle of changing your payroll information of federal and state identification numbers. You want to change but don't want anything complex.

The good news is you can convert your business structure to an LLC without too much trouble. It's easier and less costly than you may think.

Your first step is to understand what your state requires. This usually involves the filing of Articles of Conversion, which is a two- or three-page document and not a lot of questions. A small fee may be required, which you pay and then file the Articles. Voila! You are now an LLC.

Transferring your entity to the LLC is a seamless transaction. You can do this yourself or hire an attorney to process the paperwork for you. Hiring an attorney is obviously the more expensive option. The result is that your business is an LLC treated as a sole proprietorship, partnership, or corporation. Your payroll numbers as well as your federal and state identification numbers stay the same.

Let's go through each of the business structures as if you've decided to transition from the existing business structure to the same business structure but in the bunker of an LLC.

 If you are changing your business structure in addition to switching to an LLC, there is more to consider.

Sole Proprietorship

If you are now operating as a sole proprietorship, I suggest you convert as soon as you can. You are operating your business without protection, and there's really no reason not to when converting is so easy.

You file the Articles of Conversion, pay a small fee, and your business is now operating as an LLC. You simply transfer your business assets to the new LLC in exchange for the membership interest. You are the owner, but now act as a member owning the LLC. Pretty easy, right? Your assets, which were appropriately titled to your sole proprietorship, transfer to your LLC.

Let people know your business is now an LLC. Change your bank account, letterhead, business cards, and such, to let creditors know you are now an LLC.

By the way, when filing yearly taxes, you will fill out and include a Schedule C form that has the new name (if it changed) along with the designation, LLC. Nothing else changes.

Partnerships

This also is a very easy transition. The partners will file the Articles of Conversion and your partnership becomes an LLC and is treated as a partnership. This event is completely non-taxable. Everything stays the same, although you might want to change some of the language in the operating agreement. Partner percentages remain the same, the payroll and federal identification numbers remains the same, allocations and distributions go according to the old agreement, which now applies to the LLC. The transfer is very seamless but well worth it.

Corporations

If you are operating as a C Corporation or an S Corporation, you would file the Articles of Conversion and your business becomes an LLC treated as a corporation. You, in effect, have transferred your assets to the LLC in exchange for the membership interest in the LLC treated as a corporation. The corporation is still taxed as a C or S, but you are now an LLC treated as a corporation.

PART SIX

OTHER WAYS TO USE LLCS

REAL ESTATE

Titling real estate in an LLC is a good strategy for protecting personal assets. For example, if you own a building and rent it out, your tenants are potential creditors should something happen to them on your property. However, if the building is titled in an LLC, and tenants or customers sue, they will be limited to what is bunkered inside the LLC.

Owners of rental properties have liability insurance to cover these (and more) situations. However, if a judgment exceeds the liability insurance and you are operating as an LLC, judgments cannot be satisfied with personal assets. Likewise, if you are sued personally, the LLC safeguards assets within the LLC from any personal judgments. You cannot protect yourself against your own negligence, but pretty much everything else is shielded.

Ownership of real estate is best handled by a partnership or a single member LLC. Both-structures are pass through entities, which means they won't experience double taxation. All the benefits of owning real estate flows to the owner.

The worst structure is a corporation, whether it's a C corporation or an S corporation. When a C corporation owns the real estate, the income and expenses are reported at the corporate level. This means owners don't reap the benefits of including depreciation losses on personal tax returns. This tax structure also makes it difficult to sell real estate. It is double taxation in that the sale is taxed at the corporate level and proceeds distributed to the owner are taxed again.

The S Corporation is not much better. While there is no double tax, you cannot depreciate property to the extent the corporation has borrowed from a lender to buy the property. You lose one of the most valuable real estate deductions you have, which is depreciation.

ESTATE PLANNING AND ASSET PROTECTION

It is common for families to use family limited liability companies to hold the family assets, including the business, real estate or other investments. A family limited liability company is a holding company owned by parents who retain control of the LLC. Their children are then issued interests in the LLC with various rights and benefits but without control.

The purpose of a family limited liability company relates mostly to estate planning and asset protection. While a discussion of estate planning and LLC's is beyond our purpose here, it is a good technique whereby minority ownership of the family LLC is transferred to intended heirs such as children and grandchildren. The value of the interests transferred to children and grandchildren are now out of the parents' estate. The transfer is tax efficient as value without control is reduced for gift tax purposes. The result is a reduction in estate tax.

By doing this, asset protection is also accomplished. The assets within the family limited liability company have protection against creditors. Additionally, the interests of the children and grandchildren are protected as they lack control, and therefore, are more resilient to creditor claims.

Consider this example. Bill and Kathy are married with an estate of $26,000,000. This includes a business, investments assets, and personal property. They have two children. They transfer their business and investment assets, worth $15,000,000 to the family limited liability company. Bill and Kathy gift $10,000,000 worth of membership interests to their kids. Because of the lack of control, the $10,000,000 has a 30% discount, or a worth of $7,000,000. Bill and Kathy would pay a gift tax on $7,000,000 rather than the full $10,000,000. By doing this, they have transferred a good portion of their family assets to the children on a discounted basis. This portion will not be included in their estate yet can grow and appreciate outside of the estate.

VEHICLES, BOATS AND AIRPLANES

Creditors can seize vehicles, boats and airplanes, as well as sue you for things that go wrong. To ensure better protection from claims, you can title them to an LLC. Owners may or may not title vehicles their children use to an LLC, whereas airplanes and boats are regularly titled to LLCs. Airplanes and boats carry a lot of liability; therefore, transferring these assets to an LLC helps protect you from liability claims. While this is no substitute for adequate insurance, the LLC can help.

GLOSSARY

Allocations

Allocations refer to the amount of an LLC's earnings or loss attributed to the members within the LLC.

Articles of Organization (aka Articles of Formation)

Formal documentation that conveys an LLC into legal formation. Documentation is filed with the state, usually with the Secretary of State's office.

Charging Order

A court-authorized lien placed on distributions made from a business. A charging order allows a creditor to garnish distributions to recoup money owed to them by a member or owner of a business entity.

Corporations, C and S

A business entity that can be taxed wholly independently from its owners and shareholders. The C corporation's standard legal form is Subchapter C of the IRS tax code. The members of an S corporation are subject to pass-through taxation as opposed to having the corporation taxed as an independent entity.

Distributions

In the context of LLCs, distributions refer to profits given to the LLC's members in the form of cash or some other asset. Distributions are separate from allocations. An LLC owner, through the allocation of profits, may be allocated a portion of profits on which he must pay taxes, but this doesn't necessarily mean he receives the same amount in distributions. See **"Phantom Income."**

DBA (Doing Business As)

A fictitious name used by a business that operates under a name that is not their legal name. DBAs are usually used by sole proprietors or partnerships.

Dual Entity Strategy

A strategy employed by a corporation seeking to convert into an LLC, whereby the corporation remains legally existent, and the LLC leases the corporation's assets for operational use.

Dual Protection

A unique feature of an LLC whereby not only are the members limited in their personal liability for the actions of the company, but the company is also immune from the personal actions of its members.

Fair Market Value (FMV)

A selling price for an asset upon which both seller and buyer can agree.

Manager-Managed

A type of management arrangement in which the LLC members elect or hire a manager to conduct affairs on behalf of the business. The manager may or may not be a member of the LLC.

Member-Managed

A type of management arrangement in which the LLC members manage the business on their own through voting and designating various responsibilities.

Operating Agreement

A legally binding document that defines ownership roles, responsibilities, authorizations, and profit-shares in an LLC.

Partnership

Two or more individuals who go into business together. Members of a partnership may be personally liable for debts and legal judgments incurred against the business.

Pass-Thru Taxation

A system whereby a business entity is not taxed independently. Profits are allocated and taxed on the business's owners' individual tax returns.

Phantom Income

A situation that occurs when a member of an LLC is taxed on income that was never distributed. For example, a two-member LLC achieves $500,000 in profits one year, and $400,000 is invested back into the business, and only $100,000 is distributed equally among the partners, $50,000 apiece. Each partner will still have a tax liability of $250,000 even though they only received $50,000 in distributions.

Professional Service LLC

LLCs available in some states that are specifically designed for licensed professionals such as accountants, doctors, dentists, lawyers, or engineers. Professional service LLCs often aren't guaranteed as much insulation from personal liability as standard LLCs.

Registered Agent

Registered agents are named in the LLC's Articles of Organization and personify the LLC, acting as its representative to the outside world. If an LLC is sued, for example, until the registered agent is served the legal paperwork, the suit will not be formally recognized.

Self-Employment Tax

The combination of Social Security and Medicare taxes collected on individuals who receive certain types of income such as LLC business profits. These taxes are higher than the Social Security and Medicare taxes paid by wage earners because the self-employed individual is paying both their half of the obligation as well as the half normally paid by an employer.

Sole Proprietorship

The simplest form of business to form, but the individual's personal assets are at risk for any liabilities incurred by the company.

ABOUT THE AUTHOR

Chris formed Cassidy CPA in 2000. She is a member of the California Bar and US Tax Court. She has extensive experience in litigation with the San Francisco District Attorney and Public Defense's office and years of experience as a CPA with KPMG (Klynveld Peat Marwick Goerdeler), a prestigious tax advisory service company. Her legal background makes her uniquely qualified to provide not only tax services, but also expert advice on business restructuring and planning. She earned her BA from University of California, Berkeley, a JD from the University of San Francisco School of Law, and an LLM (Master of Law degree) from New York University Graduate School of Law.

She is a member of American Institute of Certified Public Accountants (AICPA), South Carolina Association of CPAs, the State Bar of California, and the American Bar Association.

Made in the USA
Middletown, DE
15 November 2021

52340589R00036